STEPS TO VICTORY

3

GW00480655

STEPS TO

3

VICTORY

ROBERT MORRIS

STUDY GUIDE

GATEWAY® PRESS

ISBN: 978-1-951227-34-0 Paperback
ISBN: 978-1-951227-35-7 eBook

We hope you hear from the Holy Spirit and receive God's richest blessings
from this book by Gateway Press. We want to provide the highest quality
resources that take the messages, music, and media of Gateway Church
to the world. For more information on other resources from Gateway
Publishing, go to gatewaypublishing.com.

Gateway Press, an imprint of Gateway Publishing
700 Blessed Way
Southlake, Texas 76092
gatewaypublishing.com

21 22 23 24   5 4 3 2 1

CONTENTS

STOP BELIEVING LIES

We open a door to the enemy when we believe his lies. Satan has been trying to gain access to our lives through lies since the beginning. The door to the enemy stays closed when our words and thoughts align with the truth of God's Word.

ENGAGE

Name three bands or musical artists and say that you have seen them live in concert. Choose two of them that will be the truth and one a lie. See if the people in your group can guess the lie.

WATCH

Watch "Stop Believing Lies."

- Think about the parts of your life that seem to always be problematic. Is it possible that you are believing a lie?
- Look for ways you may be able to align your thought life better with God's Word.

(If you are not able to watch this teaching on video, read the following. Otherwise, skip to the **Talk** section after viewing.)

READ

A woman once asked me for prayer because the enemy (the devil) was lying to her. I asked why we needed to pray if she knew it was the enemy and she knew he was lying. We agreed the real issue was that she believed those lies. This happens to all of us. We are in warfare, and the enemy's greatest tactic is deception. In Genesis 3, Satan in the form of the serpent had to get Eve to believe a lie before she sinned.

While in the emergency room as child, I overheard a nurse say I would probably be back in the emergency room most of my adult life because I was accident prone. I believed that lie. I believed it as a child when I had different kinds of accidents and injuries. I still believed it in 2007 when I stepped in a hole while on vacation. My ankle socket was completely shattered and had to be rebuilt surgically, and I broke my foot. Disc golf isn't a contact sport. It's not supposed to be, anyway.

I tried to find creative, yet honest, answers to the question "What happened?" This was one accident in a line of many. From a tricycle crash, to being hit by a car, to a motorcycle crash, I had a lot of accidents and injuries that helped to perpetuate this lie. As I was recovering from that accident in 2007, I prayed about this. I asked the Lord if I had opened a door to the enemy since I've had so many accidents. He said, "Yes because you believed a lie."

The way to know you have believed a lie is that you aren't surprised. Maybe you've heard someone say they aren't surprised by their cancer diagnosis because their father had cancer. Sometimes we forget that we've been adopted into a new family. Satan will say these things are normal, but they are not normal for Kingdom children.

> Now the serpent was more cunning than any beast of the field which the Lord God had made. And he said to the woman, "Has God indeed said, 'You shall not eat of every tree of the garden'?" And the woman said to the serpent, "We may eat the fruit of the trees of the garden; but of the fruit of the tree which *is* in the midst of the garden, God has said, 'You shall not eat it, nor shall you touch it, lest you die.'" Then the serpent said to the woman, "You will not surely die" (Genesis 3:1-4).

Do you see the lie? God told her she would surely die, but the serpent said she wouldn't. I hope you'll think about what lie(s) you have believed. You may have even spoken those words. But do you still believe them?

The Sins that We Continue

If we persist in a sin that we know is a sin, we open the door to the enemy. One of the most common sins we persist in is unforgiveness. In order for us to be forgiven for our sins, we must forgive those who sin against us. Satan wants us to continue in sin so that he has an open door into our lives to steal, kill, and destroy. One way to close the door to the enemy is by forgiving others.

If we keep rehearsing an offense in our heads, then we haven't forgiven. The apostle Paul said it this way:

> Now whom you forgive anything, I also *forgive*. For if indeed I have forgiven anything, I have forgiven that one for your sakes in the presence of Christ, lest Satan should take advantage of us; for we are not ignorant of his devices (2 Corinthians 2:10–11).

To forgive means to release. If you are rehearsing something in your mind, then you haven't forgiven. Satan lies to us and tells us that we can't release another person because then nothing will happen to them. First of all, it is God's responsibility to deal with them. Secondly, something will happen to *you* if you don't forgive. You'll be stuck. You may say, "But they were wrong!" Exactly. You don't forgive people for doing the right thing. Forgiveness is for wrong-doing. The same way God in Christ forgave you.

The Words that We Speak

> Death and life *are* in the power of the tongue,
> And those who love it will eat its fruit (Proverbs 18:21).

Proverbs 18:21 is a familiar verse, but some people take it to an extreme. They think their words have creative power. They don't. Only God has creative power. We have to choose whether the words we speak agree with the One who has creative power or the one who has destructive power. Proverbs 6:2 tells us that the words we speak can ensnare us. Are you in bondage because of the words of your own mouth? The good news is that words can also be broken.

Practice this at home. If you hear your children call themselves stupid, break those words. Speak over them that they have the mind of Christ. Don't let them stay in bondage to their words. How can just saying something make a difference? Because we speak from our hearts (Matthew 12:34). If your child has believed a lie in their heart, use the truth of God's Word to replace that lie so they can be freed.

The Thoughts that We Think

If you are wondering how a simple thought can have an impact, then Proverbs 23:7 teaches us, "For as he thinks in his heart, so *is* he." It is amazing how often we believe something about ourselves and it becomes truth.

> And you shall know the truth, and the truth shall make you free (John 8:32).

If the truth makes you free, what does a lie do? A lie will hold you in bondage. Consider when the children of Israel sent spies to stake out the land. Twelve spies went, but there were two different reports. Ten spies came back with a bad report; only two came back with a good report. Let's read the bad report:

> And they gave the children of Israel a bad report of the land which they had spied out, saying, "The land through which we have gone as spies is a land that devours its inhabitants, and all the people whom we saw in it are men of great stature. There we saw the giants (the descendants of Anak came from the giants); and we were like grasshoppers in our own sight, and so we were in their sight" (Numbers 13:32-33).

These 10 spies saw themselves as grasshoppers, so their enemy saw also them as grasshoppers. Every lie contains some truth. The truth is there were giants in the land. But the Kingdom truth is that giants are not a problem to God. He can take down a giant with a boy and slingshot. We have to remember that Satan will fabricate evidence to back up his lies. It doesn't matter what the evidence says—it only matters what the Word of God says.

NOTES

_____

_____

_____

_____

_____

_____

_____

_____

_____

_____

_____

_____

_____

_____

_____

_____

_____

_____

TALK

These questions can be used for group discussion or personal reflection.

Question 1

Is there any lie you have believed about your marriage, children, health, or finances?

_____

_____

_____

_____

Question 2

Are there any sins that have continued in your life because of a lie you believed?

_____

_____

_____

_____

Question 3
What word(s) have you allowed to stand that do not agree with God's Word?

_____

_____

_____

_____

Question 4
What changes do you plan to make now that lies have been exposed?

_____

_____

_____

_____

PRAY

If studying alone, ask the Holy Spirit to reveal the truth about Himself to you. If in a group, take some time to pray for each other as you think about the truths discussed in this session.

EXPLORE

Do you want to go deeper with this teaching? Here are some additional things to think about, pray for, or write about in your journal throughout the next week.

Key Quote

> *If the truth sets you free, what does a lie do? It keeps you in bondage.*

In what ways might a lie keep you in bondage?

_____

_____

_____

_____

_____

Key Verses

Proverbs 6:2; 18:21; 23:7; John 8:32

What truths stand out to you as you read these verses?

_____

_____

_____

What is the Holy Spirit saying to you through these Scriptures?

_____

_____

_____

Key Question

What thoughts have you kept thinking that are contrary to God's thoughts about you?

Key Prayer

Heavenly Father, thank You for Your truth, and thank You for revealing the lies of the enemy. I renounce those lies. I ask You to forgive me for the sin in which they kept me bound. I confess Your truth over my life. I am a new creation. Old things have passed away. Thank You for making me new. I forgive those who hurt me and spoke lies over my life, just as You forgave me. In Jesus' name, Amen.

2

STAY IN THE WORD

God made us spirit, soul, and body. He created our spirits to relate to Him. Through Jesus, we have the finished work of grace in our spirits and the progressive work of grace in our souls. Transformation happens when we let God's Word change our souls.

ENGAGE

What is the most out-of-character thing you've ever done?

RECAP

In the previous session, we discovered that we can find ourselves in bondage because of lies we have believed. These lies can keep us in sin, convince us to speak negative words of agreement with the enemy, and are toxic to our thought lives unless we get our perspective from God's Word.

Have you noticed some relief in your life now that some lies have been exposed?

WATCH

Watch "Stay in the Word."

- Think about the times you have walked away from the Father and maybe didn't even realize it.
- Look for perspectives that will help you as you read your Bible.

(If you are not able to watch this teaching on video, read the following. Otherwise, skip to the **Talk** section after viewing.)

READ

Years ago, Debbie and I were out shopping and had our daughter, Elaine, with us. Elaine was three at the time. Debbie asked me to watch Elaine so she could go try on some clothes in the dressing room. I knew from the tone of her request that she was really saying, "Don't lose her while I'm in the dressing room." We have two older kids that I watched before and didn't lose ... often. In a few minutes, I looked up, and Elaine was gone, of course. I found her outside of the store with a couple of older ladies who happened to see a three-year-old walking alone by their bench in the mall. They asked what she was doing, and she replied, "I go shopping." I thanked them for stopping her, as they glared at me. We hurried back to the store so we could be there when Debbie got out of the dressing room. We didn't make it. Debbie was standing there at the entrance with that same glare I just left.

Why did Elaine walk away from her father? Was she being malicious or sinful? Not at all. She was simply following an impulse. "I go shopping." She did the thing that popped into her mind. This is exactly what the Bible teaches that baby Christians will do. They haven't learned to renew their minds, so they walk away from the Father for a moment while chasing an impulse. As we develop a habit of staying in the Word, not just occasionally but continually reading the Bible, we learn to curb these impulses and stay close to our Father.

Not understanding how we are made is why Christians have problems. We are three parts: spirit, soul, and body. God created our bodies, and when He breathed His Spirit into us, we became living souls. God created our spirits to relate to Him, and He created our souls to relate to Him and His creation. When Adam and Eve sinned, their spirits died. They began to relate to God only through their souls. When we are born again, our spirits are made alive, and we can relate to God spirit to spirit.

The Soul Is Selfish

Soul means self. The soul is mind, will, and emotions. It is what we think, what we desire, and what we feel. Anything that is soulish is selfish. We came into this world with a dead spirit and for years only related to God with our minds. This is why there are so many unhealthy religious sects. Many groups have formed over the years based only on what their own intellects can figure out.

Let's do a little study on the mind. Your mind is the best computer on this earth today. There will never be a computer invented that will surpass the human mind. Your mind knows everything that you have ever seen, heard, or experienced and has categorized it. Now you may be asking, "Well, where is it, because I can't remember anything?" It is in your subconscious. When you walk into a room, your mind will immediately ask if you have even been in a similar room. It will then scan the room and determine you have been in 493 rooms like this before. That is how we get déjà vu. This is how you can meet someone and not like them. Your mind tells you that you have met people like them before and one of them pulled your gym shorts down in seventh grade.

Why am I telling you about your mind? Because every time you come up against something that causes you stress or tension, your mind asks if it has ever dealt with that kind of situation. Then your mind will tell you how to respond. The Bible calls this a stronghold. Strongholds of lust, anger, pride, and so forth, all work like this. They want to rule your response. Addictions work the same way. A situation arises that feels familiar, and your mind might say, "I need a drink."

This is why it is so important to renew your mind through the Word of God. Eventually you will have to face a challenge, and your mind will remember how you overcame a similar challenge the last time. Your mind will tell you that it is time to get into the Word and call someone for prayer. The Word will change the way you address strongholds.

The Soul Must Submit to the Spirit

It was said to her, "The older shall serve the younger" (Romans 9:12).

Your soul has been living longer than your spirit, since your spirit was born (came alive) when you got saved. The soul resists when the spirit comes alive and wants to take over. We are feeding either our soul or our spirit by what we read, look at, or listen to.

I got saved at 19 years old. Until then, I followed what I thought and felt and went after the things I thought were best for me. My spirit then came alive and told my soul it was now in charge. My soul responded, "Not without a fight." They have been fighting ever since. The more I spend time in the Word, however, the more often my spirit takes the lead over my soul. The more I get into the Word, the more I understand and live the truth of James 1:21:

Therefore lay aside all filthiness and overflow of wickedness, and receive with meekness the implanted word, which is able to save [make complete] your souls.

This is just one of many Scriptures that deal with the converting of our souls. It isn't talking about eternal salvation, but the changing and renewing of our mind, will, and emotions. These Scriptures help us make the right decision when our spirits and souls

disagree. The spirit will tell me to forgive my wife and turn the
other cheek, but my soul will tell me I need to give her a piece of
my mind. Obviously the spirit is right, but how can we make those
right choices more often? The most practical application is to ask
ourselves a simple question: Do the things we watch and read
feed the soul or the spirit? It is amazing how much we read on the
internet and how little we read the Bible. Then we wonder why we
don't have strength when we are tempted.

David talked to his soul. He told his soul not to be discour-
aged. He told his soul to bless God. He told his soul to be quiet.
Psalm 131:2 is a great example of this:

> Surely I have calmed and quieted my soul,
> Like a weaned child with his mother;
> Like a weaned child *is* my soul within me.

David told his soul to calm down and be quiet. His soul listened
because it was like a weaned child. You wean a child by moving
from milk to solid food. The apostle Paul explained this very thing
to the church in Corinth in 1 Corinthians 3:1–2:

> And I, brethren, could not speak to you as to spiritual *people* but
> as to carnal, as to babes in Christ. I fed you with milk and not with
> solid food; for until now you were not able *to receive it,* and even
> now you are still not able.

It is so important that the soul be fed the solid food of the Word. It is also very important where you go to church. You need to be in a place where the preacher preaches the Bible and not good opinions. Good opinions don't help—Good News helps. What does a child do when being weaned? They cry and throw a fit. Do you know why children respond that way, though? It is because they think the parent is trying to kill them by removing the only food source they have ever known. The soul responds to weaning the same way. The difference is, the soul *is* actually being killed. Selfish thoughts, desires, and feelings need to die.

The Soul Must Die

> For the word of God *is* living and powerful, and sharper than any two-edged sword, piercing even to the division of soul and spirit, and of joints and marrow, and is a discerner of the thoughts and intents of the heart (Hebrews 4:12).

What we think, want, and feel doesn't matter. It's what the Word of God says that matters. The Word of God divides between what we think, want, and feel and what God thinks, wants, and feels. The Word of God is like a sword. God wants to kill selfish thoughts, desires, and feelings that are killing you. We must pick up our cross daily to have victory. This happens when we let the Word transform our souls. Then God can fill your heart with what He thinks about you, what He desires for you, and what He feels about you.

God doesn't want to kill you; He wants to kill what is killing you. God wants soulish, selfish thoughts, desires, and feelings to die because they only lead to death. I once heard a preacher say that Jesus went to the cross so we wouldn't have to. That's true for eternal salvation, but we still have a cross. In fact, Jesus said that in order to follow Him we would have to take up our crosses daily (Luke 9:23). To live an overcoming life, we have to crucify the flesh every day.

In order to walk in abundant life, we must die daily to our selfish desires. The key to this is staying in the Word. God doesn't just want us to read the Bible every day, He wants the Bible to read us. He wants to speak to us through His Word so we can make healthy decisions and overcome the trials we will face. I close every sermon at Gateway Church with the same question: "What is the Holy Spirit saying to you through this message?" We should ask ourselves a similar question when we read the Bible: "What is the Holy Spirit saying to me through this passage?" If you want to walk in victory, you are going to have to stop believing lies and stay in the Word.

NOTES

TALK

These questions can be used for group discussion or personal reflection.

Question 1

Think about the last challenging situation you faced. Did you respond according to your mind, will, and emotions or by the truth of God's Word?

_____

_____

_____

_____

Question 2

How can you reprioritize your day so that you can read the Bible regularly?

_____

_____

_____

_____

Question 3

What are some things you say about yourself that disagree with what God says about you?

_____

_____

_____

_____

Question 4

Is there anything you consistently feed on from which you should be weaning off?

_____

_____

_____

_____

Question 5

Have you found a particular Scripture that is special to you and gives you strength in the tough times? What is it, and why is it so special?

_____

_____

_____

_____

PRAY

If studying alone, ask the Holy Spirit to reveal the truth about Himself to you. If in a group, take some time to pray for each other as you think about the truths discussed in this session.

EXPLORE

Do you want to go deeper with this teaching? Here are some additional things to think about, pray for, or write about in your journal throughout the next week.

Key Quote

> *Good opinions don't help—Good News helps.*

What are some people's opinions about you that bother you? How might you overcome them?

_____

_____

_____

_____

_____

Key Verses

Hebrews 4:12–13; Luke 9:23; James 1:21; Psalm 131:2

What truths stand out to you as you read these verses?

_____

_____

_____

What is the Holy Spirit saying to you through these Scriptures?

_____

_____

_____

Key Question

Are you feeding your spirit and starving your soul, or are you feeding your soul and starving your spirit?

Key Prayer

Heavenly Father, I surrender my thoughts, my desires, and my feelings to You. Please keep drawing me to Your Word so I can know Your thoughts about me, Your desires for me, and Your feelings toward me. I am so grateful that You are for me and want me to walk in victory. In Jesus' name, Amen.

3

START GOING TO CHURCH

As the body of Christ, we need to come together for edification, direction, and protection. We need to go to church to experience God's presence, God's power, and God's people.

ENGAGE

If someone made a documentary of your life, what would be your favorite scene?

RECAP

In the previous session, we learned about the dangers of following our selfish thoughts, desires, and feelings and how God's Word will give us victory over them. Only His Word can separate our thoughts from God's and help us take up our cross daily.

Since the last session, have you been able to prioritize time to read the Bible? If so, how has that affected you?

WATCH

Watch "Start Going to Church."
- Consider why you do or do not go to church regularly.
- Keep an open mind as the importance of going to church is discussed.

(If you are not able to watch this teaching on video, read the following. Otherwise, skip to the **Talk** section after viewing.)

READ

One Sunday morning, a man told his wife he wasn't going to church with his family that day. He even gave her three reasons to prove his case. He said, "I am not going because I don't like that building. I never have. I also don't like the people. And those people don't like me. I can tell." His wife responded, "Honey, you have to go, and I will give you three reasons why. I've gotten up and I'm going. The kids have gotten up and they're going. And you're the pastor, and those people are expecting you to be there."

Going to church can be a struggle for everyone—even pastors. But there are three reasons why going to church is so important in order to have victory in your life.

God's Presence

God is everywhere, but His manifest presence is His "made-known" presence that happens when we come together. When the whole body comes together, and we worship God, His presence is strong. When we don't go to church, we miss out on the corporate anointing. Church is where God's presence shows up. The presence of God distinguishes the Church from every other organization in the world. Moses received the pattern for the Tabernacle from heaven because God desires to be with His people.

> And let them make Me a sanctuary, that I may dwell among them.... And there I will meet with you, and I will speak with you from above the mercy seat, from between the two cherubim which *are* on the ark of the Testimony, about everything which I will give you in commandment to the children of Israel (Exodus 25:8, 22).

God wants His people to gather so they can experience His presence and hear His voice together. Jesus confirmed this in Matthew 18:20 when He said, "For where two or three are gathered in My name, I am there in the midst of them." I bet you can remember some worship services where the presence of God was real and life-changing. When His Body comes together to worship Him, His presence is so much stronger.

When God got angry at the Israelites in the wilderness, He told Moses that He wasn't going with them to the Promised Land. He was just going to send an angel. Moses' response was, "If you aren't going to go, then I don't want to go." Moses went on to ask, "If Your presence doesn't go with us, how will we be different than any other people in the world?" (See Exodus 33:15–16). God's presence is the only thing that makes us different. His presence is what makes the

Church different from every other organization in the world. The Church is God's House, and we need to show up because He does.

God's Power

> Again I say to you that if two of you agree on earth concerning anything that they ask, it will be done for them by My Father in heaven. For where two or three are gathered together in My name, I am there in the midst of them (Matthew 18:19-20).

Many people quote these verses separately and never connect them. The reason what you ask is done is because you have gathered in His name, so He is right there with you. If His presence is there, His power is there. How many people are missing out on the power of God they so desperately need because they are not going to church?

I grew up going to church at least three times each week. We were there Sunday morning, Sunday night, and Wednesday night. That wasn't counting the weeks where we had Tuesday visitation, Thursday night Bible study, or Saturday morning men's breakfast. Now I'm not advocating for that. I'm not even advocating for every weekend. I know life gets busy, and you may have to travel or have events with your kids. But for your own sake, you should be in church as often as possible to connect with God's power. God's power is exponential. Deuteronomy 32:30 teaches that one can put 1,000 to flight and two can put 10,000 to flight. You need to be with other believers so that we can all experience the victory of God's exponential power that comes with His manifest presence.

There is a real problem today with people approaching church like a restaurant. They decide what they are in the mood for that day, and that is where they go. The issue with that is they are missing out on what the church is designed to be. Churches do not exist so we can bounce around and take the best of each one. Churches are places in which to be planted so you can flourish, stay fresh, and bear fruit (see Psalm 92:13). It is God's power that produces these great things in our lives.

God's People

You may be wondering why you would need God's people if you already have His presence and His power. You need them because His presence and power flows through His people. Some go through life saying, "It's just me and God, and I don't need anyone else." Besides being grammatically incorrect, they are theologically incorrect. All of God's creation was good except for the man being alone. At the end of every day of creation, God said it was good. That was until the day He made Adam. He said, "That's not good—I can do better than that." Then came Eve.

Since many of us don't have any Jewish heritage in our families, we don't realize how truly incredible it is to be called the people of God. We have been grafted in and must learn this truth. As Peter put it, we once were not a people but are now the people of God (1 Peter 2:10). He was quoting a passage from Hosea:

> Then I will say to *those who were* not My people,
> "You *are* My people!"
> And they shall say, "*You are* my God!" (Hosea 2:23).

It is good to be part of the people of God. Jesus reiterated this when He was asked what is the most important commandment. He said it was obviously to love the Lord with your heart, mind, soul, and strength. He went on to say there was a second that was equally important: to love your neighbor as yourself. On these two commandments hang all the Law and the Prophets, which is the entire Bible (Matthew 22:36-40).

Why do we need God's people? Paul explained this to the Corinthian church in 1 Corinthians 14:26:

> How is it then, brethren? Whenever you come together, each of you has a psalm, has a teaching, has a tongue, has a revelation, has an interpretation. Let all things be done for edification.

Edification means to be built up. Paul is saying here that we come to church to be built up by someone else's psalm, teaching, tongue, revelation, or interpretation. In other words, God is going to give someone else what you need and give you what someone else needs. And you're all going to have to come together to get it.

As great as it is to gather, we need to take it further. We need to assemble. Gathering gets us into the same room, but it doesn't necessarily assemble us. If you look at a pile of bricks, there is strength, value, and beauty in each one individually. Then when you correctly relate them all together, they become stronger, more valuable, and more beautiful. A lot of churches are just piles of bricks, but if you assemble them, you have a house. A house is where you can meet with and speak with someone.

> Not forsaking the assembling of ourselves together, as *is* the manner of some, but exhorting *one another,* and so much the more as you see the Day approaching (Hebrews 10:25).

We should be assembling together and exhorting each other more, not less. Church attendance should be going up, not down, because the Day is approaching! When the people of God come together, His presence and power are released. This is how we get victory. We stop believing lies, we renew our souls by God's Word, and we go to church to experience God's presence, power, and people.

NOTES

_____

_____

_____

_____

_____

_____

_____

_____

_____

_____

_____

_____

_____

_____

_____

_____

_____

_____

_____

_____

_____

TALK

These questions can be used for group discussion or personal reflection.

Question 1

What are your biggest obstacles to attending church?

_____

_____

_____

_____

Question 2

Can you recall a time when you experienced God's presence in a worship service?

_____

_____

_____

_____

Question 3

Do you have a testimony of God's power changing a desperate situation?

_____

_____

_____

_____

Question 4

Have you ever been edified by someone at church, or have you ever been used to edify someone else?

_____

_____

_____

_____

Question 5

How can you be part of assembling your home church?

_____

_____

_____

_____

PRAY

If studying alone, ask the Holy Spirit to reveal the truth about Himself to you. If in a group, take some time to pray for each other as you think about the truths discussed in this session.

EXPLORE

Do you want to go deeper with this teaching? Here are some additional things to think about, pray for, or write about in your journal throughout the next week.

Key Quote

> *God wants His people to gather so they can experience His presence and hear His voice together.*

Describe a time when you heard God's voice during the church's assembly.

_____

_____

_____

_____

_____

Key Verses

Psalm 92:13; Hebrews 10:25; Hosea 2:23; Exodus 33:15-16

What truths stand out to you as you read these verses?

_____

_____

_____

What is the Holy Spirit saying to you through these Scriptures?

_____

_____

_____

Key Question

What is happening in your life right now that cries out for God's presence, power, and people?

Key Prayer

Father, thank You for wanting to dwell with Your people. Thank You for allowing us to access Your presence and power. I ask that You help me stay mindful of how special it is to be part of Your people. I want to be available to receive from others, and I pray that You would use me to bless someone else. May Your Church assemble and rise up like never before and tell everyone that the Day is approaching. In Jesus' name, Amen.

LEADER'S GUIDE

The *3 Steps to Victory* Leader's Guide is designed to help you lead your small group or class through the *3 Steps to Victory* curriculum. Use this guide along with the curriculum for a life-changing, interactive experience.

BEFORE YOU MEET

- Ask God to prepare the hearts and minds of the people in your group. Ask Him to show you how to encourage each person to integrate the principles all of you discover into your daily lives through group discussion and writing in your journals.
- Preview the video segment for the week.
- Plan how much time you'll give to each portion of your meeting (see the suggested schedule below). In case you're unable to get through all of the activities in the time you have planned, here is a list of the most important questions (from the **Talk** section) for each week.

SESSION ONE

Q: Is there any lie you have believed about your marriage, children, health, or finances?

Q: What changes do you plan to make now that lies have been exposed?

SESSION TWO

Q: Think about the last challenging situation you faced. Did you respond according to your mind, will, and emotions or by the truth of God's Word?

Q: What are some things you say about yourself that disagree with what God says about you?

SESSION THREE

Q: What are your biggest obstacles to attending church?

Q: Have you ever been edified by someone at church, or have you ever been used to edify someone else?

SUGGESTED SCHEDULE

1. **Engage** and **Recap** (5 Minutes)
2. **Watch** or **Read** (20 Minutes)
3. **Talk** (25 Minutes)
4. **Pray** (10 minutes)

HOW TO USE THE CURRICULUM

The One Thing
This is a brief statement under each session title that sums up the main point—the key idea—of the session.

Engage
Ask the icebreaker question to help get people talking and feeling comfortable with one another.

Recap
At the first meeting, provide an overview of the curriculum and encourage everyone to read and prepare before each meeting.
For the following meetings, recap the previous session and invite members to talk about any opportunities they have encountered to apply what they learned.

Watch
Watch the videos (recommended).

Read
If you're unable to watch the videos, read these sections.

Talk

The questions in this curriculum are intentionally open-ended. Use them to help the group members reflect on Scripture and the truths learned in the session.

Pray

Ask members to share their concerns and then pray together. Be sensitive to the Holy Spirit and the needs of the group.

Explore

Encourage members to complete the written portion in their books before the next meeting.

KEY TIPS FOR THE LEADER

- Generate participation and discussion.
- Resist the urge to teach. The goal is for great conversation that leads to discovery.
- Ask open-ended questions—questions that can't be answered with "yes" or "no" (e.g., "What do you think about that?" rather than "Do you agree?")
- When a question arises, ask the group for their input first, instead of immediately answering it yourself.
- Be comfortable with silence. If you ask a question and no one responds, rephrase the question and wait for a response. Your primary role is to create an environment where people feel

comfortable to be themselves and participate, not to provide the answers to all of their questions.

- Ask the group to pray for each other from week to week, especially about key issues that arise during your group time. This is how you begin to build authentic community and encourage spiritual growth within the group.

KEYS TO A DYNAMIC SMALL GROUP

Relationships

Meaningful, encouraging relationships are the foundation of a dynamic small group. Teaching, discussion, worship, and prayer are important elements of a group meeting, but the depth of each element is often dependent upon the depth of the relationships among members.

Availability

Building a sense of community within your group requires members to prioritize their relationships with one another. This means being available to listen, care for one another, and meet each other's needs.

Mutual Respect

Mutual respect is shown when members value each other's opinions (even when they disagree) and are careful never to put down or embarrass others in the group (including their spouses, who may or may not be present).

Openness

A healthy small group environment encourages sincerity and transparency. Members treat each other with grace in areas of weakness, allowing each other room to grow.

Confidentiality

To develop authenticity and a sense of safety within the group, each member must be able to trust that things discussed within the group will not be shared outside the group.

Shared Responsibility

Group members will share the responsibility of group meetings by using their God-given abilities to serve at each gathering. Some may greet, some may host, some may teach, etc. Ideally, each person should be available to care for others as needed.

Sensitivity

Dynamic small groups are born when the leader consistently seeks and is responsive to the guidance of the Holy Spirit, following His leading throughout the meeting as opposed to sticking to the "agenda." This guidance is especially important during the discussion and ministry time.

Fun!

Dynamic small groups take the time to have fun. Create an atmosphere for fun and be willing to laugh at yourself every now and then!

ABOUT THE AUTHOR

Robert Morris is the senior pastor of Gateway Church, a multi-campus church in the Dallas/Fort Worth Metroplex. Since it began in 2000, the church has grown to more than 39,000 active members. His television program is aired in over 190 countries, and his radio program, *Worship & the Word with Pastor Robert*, airs on more than 850 radio stations across America. He serves as chancellor of The King's University and is the bestselling author of numerous books, including *The Blessed Life*, *Truly Free*, *Frequency*, and *Beyond Blessed*. Robert and his wife, Debbie, have been married 39 years and are blessed with one married daughter, two married sons, and nine grandchildren.

NOTES

More resources for your small group by Pastor Robert Morris!

Blessed Families Study Guide: 978-1-949399-55-4 DVD: 978-1-949399-52-3

Living in His Presence Study Guide: 978-1-945529-55-9 DVD: 978-1-949399-42-4

Lost and Found Study Guide: 978-1-945529-85-6 DVD: 978-1-949399-48-6

More Than Words Study Guide: 978-1-949399-65-3 DVD: 978-1-949399-66-0

REAL Study Guide: 978-1-945529-51-1 DVD: 978-1-949399-49-3

RELAT1ONSHIP Study Guide: 978-1-949399-54-7 DVD: 978-1-949399-51-6

The Blessed Life Study Guide: 978-0-997429-84-8 DVD: 978-1-949399-46-2

The End Study Guide: 978-1-945529-88-7 DVD: 978-1-949399-53-0

The God I Never Knew Study Guide: 978-1-945529-54-2 DVD: 978-1-949399-41-7

Why Am I Here? Study Guide: 978-1-945529-71-9 DVD: 978-1-949399-50-9

Words: Life or Death Study Guide: 978-1-945529-56-6 DVD: 978-1-949399-43-1

Beyond Blessed DVD + Discussion Guide: 978-1-949399-68-4

Eternity Study Guide: 978-1-949399-95-0 DVD: 978-1-949399-94-3

The Kings of Babylon Study Guide: 978-1-949399-98-1 DVD: 978-1-949399-97-4

A Way in the Wilderness Study Guide: 978-1-951227-01-2 DVD: 978-1-951227-00-5

Sons Not Servants Study Guide: 978-1-951227-40-1 DVD: 978-1-951227-42-5

God Is... Study Guide: 978-1-951227-37-1 DVD: 978-1-951227-39-5

3 Steps to Victory Study Guide: 978-1-951227-34-0 DVD: 978-1-951227-36-4

You can find these resources and others at www.gatewaypublishing.com